W9-CMB-798

KIWANIS INTERNATIONAL
Serving the
Children
of the World

Dinosaurs and Prehistoric Animals

Sabertooth Cat

by Helen Frost

Consulting Editor: Gail Saunders-Smith, PhD

Consultant: Jack Horner
Curator of Paleontology
Museum of the Rockies
Bozeman, Montana

Mankato, Minnesota

Pebble Plus is published by Capstone Press,
151 Good Counsel Drive, P.O. Box 669, Mankato, Minnesota 56002.
www.capstonepress.com

Printed in the United States of America

1 2 3 4 5 6 10 09 08 07 06 05

Library of Congress Cataloging-in-Publication Data
Frost, Helen, 1949–
Sabertooth cat / by Helen Frost.
p. cm.—(Pebble plus—dinosaurs and prehistoric animals)
Includes bibliographical references and index.
ISBN-13: 978-0-7368-3648-7 (hardcover)
ISBN-10: 0-7368-3648-9 (hardcover)
ISBN-13: 978-0-7368-5105-3 (softcover pbk.)
ISBN-10: 0-7368-5105-4 (softcover pbk.)
1. Smilodon—Juvenile literature. I. Title. II. Series.
QE882.C15F76 2005
569'.74—dc22 2004011091

Summary: Simple text and illustrations present sabertooth cats, their body parts, and behavior.

Editorial Credits
Martha E. H. Rustad, editor; Linda Clavel, designer; Jon Hughes, illustrator; Wanda Winch, photo researcher; Scott Thoms, photo editor

Photo Credit
Folio, Inc./Richard Cummins, 20–21

The author thanks the children's library staff at the Allen County Public Library in Fort Wayne, Indiana, for research assistance.

Note to Parents and Teachers

The Dinosaurs and Prehistoric Animals set supports national science standards related to the evolution of life. This book describes and illustrates sabertooth cats. The images support early readers in understanding the text. The repetition of words and phrases helps early readers learn new words. This book also introduces early readers to subject-specific vocabulary words, which are defined in the Glossary section. Early readers may need assistance to read some words and to use the Table of Contents, Glossary, Read More, Internet Sites, and Index sections of the book.

Table of Contents

A Prehistoric Mammal

Sabertooth cats were
prehistoric mammals.
Sabertooth cats lived more
than 1 million years ago.

Sabertooth cats lived
in grasslands and forests.

How Sabertooth Cats Looked

Sabertooth cats were about the size of a lion. They were about 3 feet (1 meter) tall.

Sabertooth cats had

two long, sharp teeth.

They had strong jaws.

Sabertooth cats had short, strong legs. They could run fast across grasslands.

What Sabertooth Cats Did

Sabertooth cats hunted
and ate other animals.
They killed their prey
with their sharp teeth.

Sabertooth cats opened their mouths wider than other animals. This helped them swallow prey.

Sabertooth cats
may have lived
in groups.

The End of Sabertooth Cats

Sabertooth cats died out about 10,000 years ago. No one knows why they all died. You can see sabertooth cat fossils in museums.

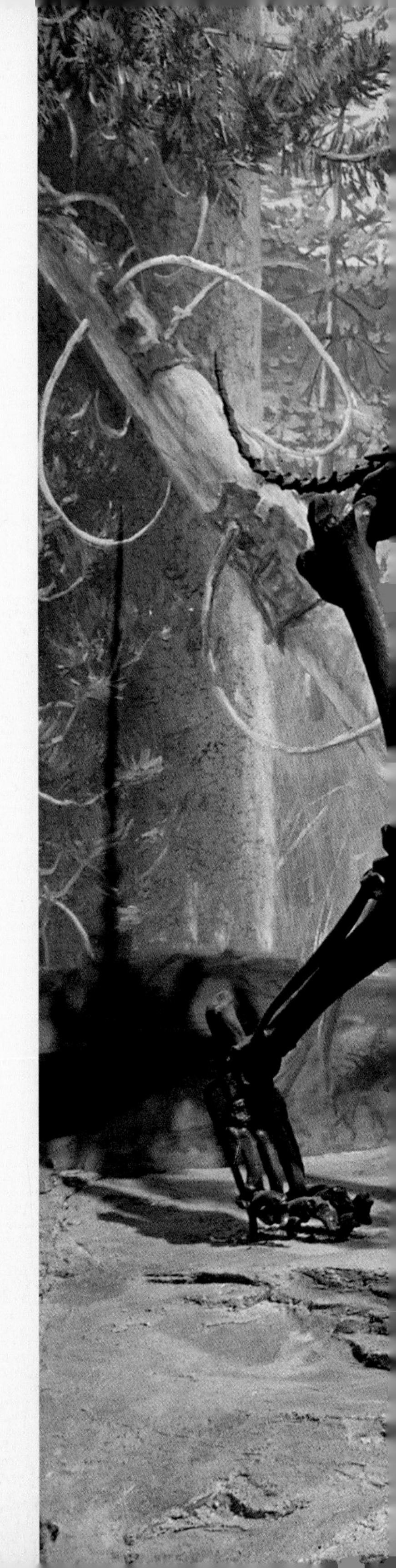

Glossary

forest—a large area covered with grass and trees

fossil—the remains or traces of an animal or a plant, preserved as rock

grassland—a large, open area where grass and low plants grow

hunt—to chase and kill animals for food; sabertooth cats hunted and ate other animals.

mammal—a warm-blooded animal with a backbone; female mammals feed milk to their young.

museum—a place where objects of art, history, or science are shown

prehistoric—very, very old; prehistoric means belonging to a time before history was written down; dinosaurs and woolly mammoths are prehistoric animals.

prey—an animal that is hunted for food

Read More

Goecke, Michael P. *Saber-toothed Cat.* Prehistoric Animals. A Buddy Book. Edina, Minn.: Abdo, 2003.

Gray, Susan Heinrichs. *Saber-toothed Cats.* Exploring Dinosaurs and Prehistoric Creatures. Chanhassen, Minn.: Child's World, 2005.

Hehner, Barbara. *Ice Age Sabertooth: The Most Ferocious Cat that Ever Lived.* New York: Crown Publishers, 2002.

Internet Sites

FactHound offers a safe, fun way to find Internet sites related to this book. All of the sites on FactHound have been researched by our staff.

Here's how:

1. Visit *www.facthound.com*
2. Type in this special code **0736836489** for age-appropriate sites. Or enter a search word related to this book for a more general search.
3. Click on the **Fetch It** button.

FactHound will fetch the best sites for you!

Index

Word Count: 120
Grade Level: 1
Early-Intervention Level: 14